Gratitude Journal

C0-BHZ-954

Kim Coles

"Choose to Live Life Out Loud"

GRATITUDE
INTENTION
FORGIVENESS
TRIUMPHS
SELF-LOVE

Actress and comedian Kim Coles
shares her personal journey of
self discovery while providing simple tools to
shorten the distance between
surviving and thriving.

Kim invites the reader to take 30 days and just focus
on being grateful, from loving yourself to celebrating
your friends & family.

The **Gratitude Journal** makes it easy to begin shifting
your focus so you can really celebrate what's
important and rise to your highest potential.

The **Gratitude Journal** is the first in the
"Open the **G.I.F.T.S**"
book series.

A Note From Me

This gratitude journal comes from part of my personal life journey. Several challenging events happened and I needed answers. I found out that gratitude was the first door to open to find those answers. This book was inspired by the steps I took to find clarity, harmony and peace. This journal is dedicated to anyone who's ever needed a little reminder that they're special and that who they are truly matters in the world. Who you "ARE" is simply enough. You don't have to "DO" anything to claim it. It's already YOURS. The world is waiting for you to open your gifts and SHINE. All you have to do is take a few steps; the road will rise up to meet you. I've been so blessed with wonderful teachers and mentors who've inspired me. It's my turn to pass it on.

My hope is that you take this journey over the next month. I know if you stick with it, you'll find there are so many things in your life you may have taken for granted. You may also discover there are so many doors available for you to just open. I've included some of my personal stories and quotes that lift me as I work on myself daily. This book is designed in a free-flowing manner so you can do as much or as little as you like and it's easy to carry, too! Please just commit to doing something each day over the next 30 days. My personal breakthrough happened on the 32nd day of writing my gratitude journal. Who knows when YOUR breakthrough will happen? Great things await you. I can feel it! I'm looking forward to hearing your story.

Special Thanks

To my mother and her sisters, who shaped me. To my father, who taught me a love of words. To my various coaches, teachers, mentors and advisors, who led me to this invaluable self-exploration work. To Denise Thackston for her indefatigable patience and hard work. And to "The Divine Spirit" that lives in me and connects us all.

PR Firm Publishing

A Division of The Personal Relationship Firm |
Authentic Speakers Agency
4263 Oceanside Blvd. Ste. 160
Oceanside, CA 92056

Designed by Denise Thackston | PR Firm
Publishing
Manufactured in the United States of
America

Why did I decide to create a gratitude journal?

Although you may know me as an actress, comedienne and TV personality, I've always been inspired to grow beyond the stage and screen. In addition to Hollywood, I'm reaching out across the country to empower and inspire others. I'm excited to launch this new chapter.

In the last few years, I've been on a personal journey to find more PURPOSE and PASSION. You know how you get that feeling that there may be MORE out there?
Or I should say more "IN" there? You know that feeling when you wonder if you're living up to your fullest human potential? This has nothing to do with WHAT we do for a living, but everything to do with WHO we are in our spirit and soul.

I truly believe the first step to being the best YOU is **GRATITUDE.**

We all experience life's ups and downs, but we can stay afloat through it all and even find joy when we remain grateful.
Gratitude is the perfect way to switch into what really matters. Plus, focusing on what already works in your life creates space for more of what you want to come in.

I've seen this work time and time again in my own life. I'm just like you. I've had relationship breakups, job disappointments and personal challenges. I remember when I was going through a very difficult personal time not too long ago and a friend told me to keep a gratitude journal for 30 days.

My life was gloomy, or so I thought. I'd gotten into the habit of complaining about what wasn't working for me. However, when I began keeping track of what was good, I had less time to focus on what I perceived as bad. My mood lightened.

Then the magic happened; I started noticing MORE to be grateful for! All kinds of wonderful opportunities presented themselves and I felt ready and grateful to receive all of them. My perspective changed and my circumstances began to change, too. It really is that simple and beautiful and magical.

" If you want to know where
your heart is,

look to where

your mind goes when it

wanders."

I did it and you can, too.
Go on, try it...
Have an ATTITUDE of GRATITUDE!
This is a workbook designed to get you going and
growing in the direction of the BEST YOU ever. You
see, I truly believe we all came here to do
something amazing and I want to see you find your
passion, live your purpose, and *SHINE!*

I'm finding it so fulfilling and heart-warming to bring
my message of the powerful journey of self-
discovery to YOU!
I'm GRATEFUL.
Let's do this together with love and ultimately
celebrate the BEST YOU ever!

This is all about the GIFT you are to the world. You were born to be special and to contribute something amazing. The gift you have inside must be opened and shared. By the way, in case you're wondering, your GIFT is what lights up your soul.

It's the thing you enjoy most and you're naturally good at it. When you think about it, you get excited and smile inside and outside. I like to say you get to **live, love and laugh OUT LOUD!** This means living to your fullest potential. I want to be your biggest cheerleader. Let's GO… **Woo Woo Woo!**

Start to make gratitude a daily habit and say thank you every single day for all the miracles that are already in your present.
Once you do, and you have to truly mean it, then the doors of the universe will swing wide open and you'll become more and more powerful at manifesting.

GRATITUDE-

I really believe when you start your day in a place of gratitude, you're setting yourself up to win! No matter what your life looks like at this moment, there's certainly *something* to be grateful for. Try writing 5 new things for 7 days and see if you don't find yourself smiling at all the good in your life. And just you wait, more is coming! As for me, I'm hoping it's a surprise residual check!
=) Woo Woo Woo!

Habits

Some people will tell you it takes 21 to 28 days to form a new habit. I don't know if anyone really knows the exact number for sure. What I do know is that at some point, we have to stop talking about being in action and simply get in action. I know this is easier said than done. I promise you I'm speaking from experience.

The 30-day journey you're about to take is the same process I did. Sometimes, when you find yourself going through a tough time, you have to take baby steps. Something as simple as reminding yourself of what you can be grateful for in your life right now is all it takes.

Why?

What you focus on tends to show up all around you. If you don't believe me, then check in with me the next time you decide to buy a new car. The moment you decide to even began considering that car, you'll see it everywhere.

For a moment you may even think to yourself, how is it possible that this area has so many makes of that model?

The car is showing up because you've given it attention. You've focused on it. Now let's look at our personal lives. If you focus on what doesn't work in your life, it continues to do just that:

NOT WORK!!

Try giving your attention to what is working
well in your life and it will continue
to get better, I promise! =)

I want to encourage you to do something different
to yield a new result. Try writing and thinking about
what you can be grateful for right now.
Do it for just 30 days; that's all I ask.

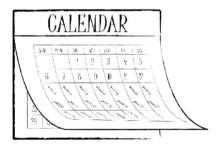

Imagine

your future

Believe

your dreams

Create

your reality!

SELF-LOVE

"Before you can love and
appreciate anyone else,
you must first love and
appreciate yourself."

Self-love is about...

Treating yourself with the same care,
tolerance, generosity,
compassion and respect

that you would give a friend.

I Love Myself

Self-love, which can also be thought of as self-esteem or self-worth, is such a tricky subject to talk about, especially since most of us aren't "factory-loaded" to love ourselves.

In my case, when I was a young girl, my parents told me not to be conceited. I suppose they were worried that if I thought too highly of myself, others would try to knock me down. I know they didn't want me to be vain, but I'm certain they wanted me to take good care of myself.

As I look back now to some of the decisions I made as a young—and not so young—woman, I can admit I didn't always love myself as fully as possible. My lack of self-love and self-worth manifested itself in so many areas of my life, including the men I chose to date, the way I treated my body and even the career choices I declined.

Today, I understand there's a big difference between being "full of yourself" and loving yourself, and the latter is critically important to being able to live the kind of life you want to live.

Lucille Ball was right when she said, "Love yourself first and everything else falls into line. You really have to love yourself to get anything done in this world."

I'm very conscious now of the value of self-love, even though it doesn't always come naturally to me. I still need to work at it, flex that muscle, so to speak...but I make time for self-worth exercises because I understand that only by loving myself will I attract the people and opportunities that truly make my heart sing.

"CHANGE

Your outlook...alter

Your outcomes."

Here's my list of the things I wrote to help me nuture self-love and remind me of my own self-worth:

KIM'S LIST!

1. Read books about self-love.

2. Meditate daily to stay connected to the Divine.

3. Set an appointment for my annual checkup that I've been putting off.

4. Eat more veggies and cut out fried foods for 5 days this month.

5. Drink more water this week.

6. Make myself a candelit tropical-scented bath.

List 10 things you love about yourself.
I give you full permission to list everything that's
amazing, wonderful and fabulous!

<u>My LIST!</u>

1.

2.

3.

4.

5.

Self-love

Keep going and don't be shy about how
fabulous you truly are! If you get stuck, ask people in
your inner circle what they love about you. I think
you'll be surprised and delighted!

6.

7.

8.

9.

10.

<u>Today I'm proud that I...</u>

"If someone is

strong enough to bring you down,

show them you are

Strong enough to

get back up."

Family and Friends

"Family is not just about

the people you are born with;

it's also the people you choose!"

" Some people
come into our lives
and quickly go.
Some stay for a while
and leave footprints on our hearts.
And we are never, ever the same.
Which one are you?"

I'm blessed to know a lot of people, but my "core," those who really ground me and give me space to be my best self, are my family and few close friends. I really cherish the people with whom I can be the "most Kim." We all need that…people who accept us just the way we are, imperfections and all, and are always there when we need them.

While most people consider family to be something you're born into, I have a broader definition. I believe your family can also consist of those you've chosen to fill your "inner circle." I have both biological and non-biological family members who serve as my truth holders; if I forget who I am or start to go off on a tangent, they're there to pull me back.

I hail from a family that has a beautiful story. My ancestors were strong, smart amazing people, and I love talking to those who are still around to discover what they were like when they were younger. I've heard some of their stories 100 times…but they never get old. I look for gems from their lives that I can use in my own.

As for friends, the older I get, the more I realize that quality is truly more important than quantity. I used to think the more friends I had, the richer I was, but now I have just a handful who are truly worth their weight in gold. We tend to use the term friend rather loosely these days, e.g., Facebook Friends, when in reality a true friend is like a diamond; instead of resulting from time and pressure, friendships are built on time and shared experiences that bond you. Never underestimate the value of great friends and family.

" It's good to have money
and the things that money can buy,

But it's good,
too, to check up once in a while that
you haven't lost the things
that money can't buy."

Our personal connections are so important to our mental and emotional health. Let's take some time to honor the relationships you love most.
Here are some quotes about family and friends that always make my smile.

My Favorite Quotes!

" Real family & friends are those who walk in when others walk out."
– Walter Winchill

" A friend is someone who understands your past, believes in your future, and accepts you just the way you are."
– Unknown

My Favorite Quotes!

"What is a friend? A friend is someone with whom you dare to be yourself."
- Unknown

"Truly great friends are hard to find, difficult to leave, and impossibile to forget."
- Unknown

"Families are like fudge- mostly sweet with a few nuts."
- Unknown

List 10 people who you're blessed to have in your life and 3 words that describe each of them.

<u>My LIST!</u>

1.

2.

3.

4.

5.

Add more family and friends and why you love them!

My LIST!

6.

7.

8.

9.

10.

Share a favorite story or memory from a family member or friend that inspires you or makes you laugh.

Family Story

" How people treat you is

their karma;
how you react is

yours"!

Share a favorite story or memory from a family member or friend that inspires you or makes you laugh.

Friend Story

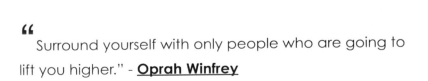

" Surround yourself with only people who are going to lift you higher." - **Oprah Winfrey**

Health

"Taking care of your health is showing appreciation to the temple you've been given."

"My body is a temple...
exercise is my prayer."

"Do what makes you happy.
Be with who makes you smile.
Laugh as much as you breathe.
Love as long as you live."

" How people treat you is

their karma;
how you react is
yours"!

When I think about my health, I realize I must be grateful for one of the most important aspects of life. Health IS wealth. We've all heard this before, but with your health intact, you can enjoy an all-around better quality of life. When you put your health first, you have the energy and ability to enjoy the life you're creating. We should seek to have all areas of health to be in good balance...physical, mental, spiritual and emotional.

This is an area that's important to me because there are choices I can make and I'm in control. For example, a lot of documentation exists on the effects of too much sugar, fat and over-processed food in your diet. Of course you want to be able to have treats, but eating greasy, fried, and sugary foods regularly isn't the most loving way to serve the beautiful body you've been given. I refuse to totally give up potato chips, but if I eat fruits and veggies most of the time, I can allow myself to indulge once in a while.

In creating any new habit, sometimes it's good to talk to an expert because we need tools to set those habits into place. An expert can get to the core of what's really going on and help to get you on a good path to your goals.

Fitness is an area that's hard for me because I have been an "all or nothing" girl. I'm either in the gym working out 6 days a week, pushing myself to the edge OR I'm sitting at home doing nothing because I'm burned out. My personal goal is to find a workout/eating plan that's doable and fun, yet still gets me to my personal goal. By the way, my personal goal is to be a foxy 80-year-old lady!

In addition to our physical health, I think we often forget about the simple things like our senses.
Things like the ability to see and hear. Imagine if you could no longer see. *Don't take anything for granted!*

We often put other people's needs ahead of our own. It's time to put yourself at the top of your own to-do list! Every small step leads to a healthier you!

KIM'S HEALTH CHECKLIST

1. Make a plan to exercise a few times a week, even if it's just a 15-minute walk.

2. Add 2 or 3 super-healthy foods to your diet, like blueberries, spinach, almonds and fish.

3. Take a multi-vitamin every single day.

4. Get 7 to 8 hours of sleep a night.

5. It's time to create your health checklist.
Remember to keep it simple!

<u>My LIST!</u>

1.

2.

3.

4.

5.

There are 86,400 seconds in a day.

How many of them will you use to honor your body? Here's a beautiful challenge: at the moment you wake up for the next 7 days, find at least one thing about your body you're grateful for.

Day 1: "This morning, I'm grateful for my sight; without it, I wouldn't be able to see the sunrise."

Day 1

There are 86,400 seconds in a day.
Today, I'm using a few of them to write
down what I'm grateful for...

Day 2

There are 86,400 seconds in a day.
Today, I'm using a few of them to write
down what I'm grateful for...

Day 3

There are 86,400 seconds in a day.
Today, I'm using a few of them to write
down what I'm grateful for...

Day 4

There are 86,400 seconds in a day.
Today, I'm using a few of them to write
down what I'm grateful for...

Day 5

There are 86,400 seconds in a day.
Today, I'm using a few of them to write
down what I'm grateful for...

Day 6

There are 86,400 seconds in a day. Today, I'm using a few of them to write down what I'm grateful for...

Day 7

" How people treat you is

their karma;
how you react is

yours"!

Finances

"An investment in knowledge always pays the best interest"!

-Benjamin Franklin

Gratitude turns what we have into *enough*"!

" Nothing is

over

until

you STOP

TRYING."

"Never give up on

something you really want.

It's difficult to wait,

but it's more difficult to

regret."

"Obstacles *are what you see when you take your* eyes off the goal."

-Vince Lombardi

"Too many people spend money *they haven't* got,

to buy things *they don't* need,

to impress people *they don't like.*"

Who among us hasn't labored to "keep up with the Jones' "?   Of course, what we didn't know was that they were broke, and struggling to keep up appearances themselves! I'm long past the stage of buying things to impress others, and have kind of gone full circle; now, I gain status by looking as cute as I can for as little as possible. "Girl, can you believe I bought this skirt for $25?" I mix and match my budget pieces with my old designer pieces and I work my look just the same!

It took me a long time to realize I need to care less about what's on my body and more about what's in my bank account. While I have years left of earning power, one of these days I'll want to "sit down," and I need to ensure I have the resources to do that. We all do. Instead of wondering how to spend money, we need to be more concerned with how we can make our money work for us by making good investments that will serve us well in the future.

No one likes to talk about money and perhaps that's the reason why a lot of us have such a troubled relationship with it. I'm quite sure my story isn't unique, since financial literacy remains something that's not taught in schools. We're taught plenty of things we may seldom or never use as an adult—like algebra, for instance—but no one bothers to explain the true value of money.

Years ago, I had a great job and made a lot of money…and I spent it all. I had all my status symbols —the Gucci purses, the Louis Vuitton luggage—and I was under the impression that those reflected my worth. What no one ever bothered to tell me was that the bright red color on the bottom of my Louboutin shoes was going to wear off!

Count your financial blessings.

Start with the simple things and watch them grow! Here are a few tips.

1. Create a B-U-D-G-E-T, which stands for:

Baby- **U**- **D**eserve **G**etting **E**very- **T**hing.

It's not about doing without; it's about taking a practical approach to living and planning for the future.

2. Track your spending for a week. Write everything down and find 2 areas where you can cut back and save.

Did you know....

Everyone has spending they can eliminate.

Example: The average coffee drinker spends $3.25 a day on coffee.

That's $16.25 a week | $65 a month | $780 a year!

How much could you save by cutting back and how could you repurpose your savings?
Use the next page to create your own financial win!

Life is an echo.

What you send out comes back.
What you sow, you reap. What you give you get.

3. Consider buying in bulk when you see items you frequently use on sale, e.g., toothpaste, paper towels and soap.

4. Empty the loose change in your purse or pocket into a savings jar.

5. Understand that your words are powerful! Eliminate phrases like, "I'm broke, I can't afford it" from your vocabulary. Try saying, "I'm temporarily financially challenged." =)

"*Imagine*
your future...
Believe
your dreams...
Create
your reality"

3 ways
I can save instead of spend!

1.

2.

3.

Random Acts of Kindness

I want you to challenge yourself to pick 3 random people and do something kind and unexpected for them.

I want to celebrate with you, so go online and tell me what you did and how the people responded.

Remember, we receive what we give out.
Who knows, you may start a movement in your own community.

Become the ripple in your own pond!

Random Acts of Kindness

Here are a few examples of easy things you can do:

1. Help a senior with his / her bags.

2. Compliment that diva who's sporting a cute natural hair style. Wink! =)

3. Offer your club card discount to the person in front of you in line who's searching like crazy to find his/hers.

4. Donate your pennies to the person who's coming up short at the check-out counter.

Random Acts of Kindness
Act 1

Random Acts of Kindness
Act 2

Random Acts of Kindness
Kindness
Act 3

Spirituality

"Before you can love and appreciate anyone else, you must first love and appreciate yourself. Honor the spirit inside of you."

I'm grateful for a spiritual connection because no matter how stressed I feel, I know I'm really only a moment away from the clarity and peace the Divine Connection provides. If I'm mindful to trust that all is well, I can get through stressful situations with greater ease.

One of ways I center myself is to take a walk in nature. I've found a simple walk outdoors can help to clear the clutter in my mind. There's a park in my neighborhood that provides a welcomed break from all the artificial noise of life. Breathing in fresh air and listening to sounds of nature are the perfect ways to reconnect with my Divine Source and myself.

Honor your spirit

Remind yourself what makes your heart sing. Take a moment and think about what really makes you smile.

For some, it's the smell of coffee in the morning or flowers on the side of their bed. It may be a random thank you note in the mail.

What are 3 things that made you smile today and why?

*Now, take a moment and honor someone else; send a postcard or note just to say I appreciate or love you!

The other way I stay connected is to meditate and pray in the morning. What a wonderful way to center myself and prepare my intention for the day.

I have to admit I don't always attend church regularly, but I'm aware that spiritual connection is available to me, always. I often stop and allow myself to feel the presence of God within me and in others. It's all around us, before, during and after the typical Sunday service.

Honor your spirit

You must find your truth so you can honor your spirit.

Recognize your power.

I am powerful, because...

Honor your spirit

You must find your truth so you can honor your spirit.

Recognize your inner beauty.

I am beautiful, because...

Honor your spirit

You must find your truth so you can honor your spirit.

Recognize your greatness.

I am great, because...

Honor your spirit

You must find your truth so you can honor your spirit.

Recognize your talent

I am really good at...

Honor your spirit

You must find your truth so you can honor your spirit.

Recognize your passion.

I really love to...

Create a list of 10 things you can do to honor your spirit.

1.

2.

3.

4.

5.

Create a list of 10 things you can do to honor your spirit.

6.

7.

8.

9.

10.

"DEAD LAST" IS
GREATER THAN

"DID NOT FINISH,"
WHICH TRUMPS

"DID NOT START"!

Imagine your future

"The future belongs to those who believe in the beauty of their dreams." – Eleanor Roosevelt

I Imagine that...

Imagination is the mother of invention.

I Imagine that...

Imagination is the mother of invention.

My Bright Random Ideas!

Imagination is the mother of invention.

Believe your dreams

"The future belongs to those who believe in the beauty of their dreams." – Eleanor Roosevelt

I Believe I can...

Sometimes you'll have to borrow someone else's faith on the road to your dream. That's OK - just don't stop dreaming.

I Believe I can...

Sometimes you'll have to borrow someone else's faith on the road to your dream. That's OK – just don't stop dreaming.

Create your reality!

"Thoughts become things...choose the good ones!"

– Mike Dooley

I will...

The world is ready and waiting on you to step up & show out!

I will...

The world is ready and waiting on you to step up & show out!

"*Imagine*
your future...

Believe

your dreams...

Create

your reality"

For more information on booking Kim Coles,
please contact:
Authentic Speakers Agency @
www.AuthenticSpeakersAgency.com

PR Firm Publishing
A Division of The Personal Relationship Firm |
Authentic Speakers Agency
4263 Oceanside Blvd. Ste. 160
Oceanside, CA 92056

Edited by Adrienne Moch
Book design by Denise Thackston | PR Firm
Publishing
Manufactured in the United States of
America

Page 64: BUDGET description by Chellie
Campbell

Copyright © 2012

ISBN 978-0-9883273-0-6

Thank you so much!

I truly hope you found this journal eye-opening and I pray you discovered some new pathways into your heart. Please keep going and growing in the direction of the best YOU ever!

I want you to keep in touch and tell me how you're doing and what gifts opened up for you. I'll also let you know when the next journal installment will be ready. Oh yes, I have so much MORE in store for you!

Reach me on twitter @kimcoles and use the #GIFTSjournal hashtag
OR Reach me on Facebook at
www.facebook.com/RealKimColes
I'd love to hear how you used this journal.

REMEMBER: Just Breathe. Just Believe. Just BE beautiful, awesome amazing you!

Actress and comedienne Kim Coles
shares her personal journey of self-discovery while
providing simple tools to shorten the distance
between surviving and thriving.

Kim invites you to take 30 days and focus on being
grateful, from loving yourself to celebrating your
friends and family. This **gratitude journal** makes it
easy to begin shifting your focus, so you can really
celebrate what's important and rise to your highest
potential.
This **gratitude journal** is the first in the
"Open the **G.I.F.T.S**" book series.

" *Choose* to Live Life Out Loud"

GRATITUDE
INTENTION
FORGIVENESS
TRIUMPHS
SELF-LOVE

www.OpenTheGifts.com
PR Firm Publishing www.PrFirmPublishing.com